T0157905

Capture Your Dreams
Through personal visioning

Michael Muthengi Makau

authorHOUSE®

AuthorHouse™ UK Ltd.
500 Avebury Boulevard
Central Milton Keynes, MK9 2BE
www.authorhouse.co.uk
Phone: 08001974150

First published by AuthorHouse   04/25/2011

ISBN: 978-1-4567-7525-4 (sc)

Scriptures quotations marked KJV are taken from *King James Version* of the bible. All rights reserved.
Scriptures quotations marked BBE are taken from *Bible in Basic English*, Copyright@2006 retrieved from www.olivetree.com. All rights reserved.
Scriptures quotations marked NASB are taken from *New American Standard Bible*, Copyright @1977 by The Lockman Foundation. All rights reserved.
Scriptures quotations marked NIV are taken from the *Holy Bible, New International Version*, Copyright @1984 by International Bible Society. All rights reserved.
Scriptures quotations marked NLT are taken from the *Holy Bible, New Living Translation*, Copyright @1996 by Tyndale House Publishers, Inx, Wheaton, Illinois 60189. All rights reserved.

Dedicated to

My wife, Martha

My life has never been the same because of you

Our son, Mukenia

You are a mark of joy in my life

Our daughter, Makena

You are radiant and a blessing to me

Contents

Acknowledgements

THIS BOOK IS THE FULFILLMENT of a dream and it would not have happened without the prayers and contribution of many people. I would like to appreciate all who were part of this book in one way or another. I am not able to mention each one of you by name but please accept my gratitude.

To Martha, my best friend and wife, who has not only prayed for me and my many dreams, but was the first to read this manuscript and has continued to encourage me to complete this project. Thanks for the many sacrifices you have made and the encouragement you have been to me.

To our children Mukenia and Makena, thanks for being there and just sitting with dad at the computer as I typed out and revised this manuscript. I hope and pray that one day you will use this book to shape your own lives.

To our dear family friend, Bev Nuthu, thanks for the challenges you have thrown my way. Thanks for reading through this manuscript and giving me very useful input to make it a better manuscript. Lastly, thanks for encouraging me to take a post-graduate course in leadership that helped shape the thoughts in this book. To your loving husband Pastor Joji for being my friend.

To Rev Dr Chip Block, our former Lead Pastor at International Christian Centre in Nairobi and a dear friend. Thanks for pulling out my hidden talents and more so, for believing in me.

To Pastor Philip Kitoto, our Senior Pastor at International Christian Centre in Nairobi and family friend. Thanks for believing in me, trusting me and encouraging me in my Christian faith.

To the former Vice Chancellor of Pan Africa Christian University, Dr Kirk Kauffeldt, you challenged us many times while at PAC University to put our thoughts on paper. I took your challenge and here it is.

To Sylvia Maina, for editing this manuscript on short notice and giving it the touch of an editor.

To my Lord Jesus Christ, without you I would be nothing. All the thoughts in this book are from you and all glory is to you.

Introduction

Imagination
A mind once stretched by a new idea, never regains its
original dimensions.
Anonymous

I HAVE WONDERED AND THOUGHT about this subject for a long time and I am convinced now more than ever before that personal visioning is what makes a person who they are. Look at any organization in the world that can be considered successful, and you will realize that it has gone through a visioning process commonly referred to as strategic planning. During this process, the organization looks at various things. It looks at where it wants to be in the next 10 years; things that are important to it (values); its strengths, opportunities, weakness & threats; the social environment it is operating in; present economic climate in the regions it operates in; present political climate and for the next few years; and the level of technology among other things. These things enable the organization to come up with a vision, mission, core values, slogan, rallying cry, strategies just to mention a few. Imagine if these organizations had individuals who have gone through the same process. The results would be amazing. The organizations would have individuals with objectives that are similar to theirs and not individuals who are only looking for a place to make money.

Why is visioning important? Like I will explain later, visioning is what keeps us going and if we are well focused in life, we can achieve our dreams. A vision makes a dream come true. A vision shapes a dream.

Let's take Steve Jobs the co-founder of Apple Inc. Mr. Jobs dropped out of college in 1976 to sell personal computers assembled in his garage. He created the first Apple computer at 21 years.[1]

Jobs' vision was to provide affordable personal computers. He had realized that there was a huge gap in the computer market. At the time, almost all computers were mainframes. They were so large that one computer could fill a room, and so costly that individuals could not afford to buy them. Jobs and Wozniak redesigned their computer with the idea of selling it to individual users.[2] Looking at the world today, I think Steve Jobs has captured his dream. A good number of people today in the world have a personal computer at home. It might not be an Apple, but the dream came true. It all started with a vision.

Martin Luther King Jr is another person that comes to mind when I think of a dream and visioning. In his famous 'I HAVE A DREAM' speech delivered on 28 August 1963, at the Lincoln Memorial Park Washington D.C, he said:

> "I have a dream that one day this nation will rise up and live out the true meaning of its creed: "We hold these truths to be self-evident, that all men are created equal."…
> I have a dream that my four little children will one day live in a nation where they will not be judged by the colour of their skin but by the content of their character…
> And when this happens, when we allow freedom ring, when we let it ring from every village and every hamlet, from every state and every city, we will be able to speed up that day when *all* of God's children, black men and white men, Jews and Gentiles, Protestants and Catholics, will be able to join hands and sing in the words of the old Negro spiritual: *Free at last! Free at last! Thank God Almighty, we are free at last!"*[3]

Martin Luther King Jr might not have seen his dream come to pass during his life but he lived fulfilled. He fought for his dream. He died fighting for this dream. His dream came to pass years later and many say that that dream was finally fulfilled in 2008 when Americans elected President Barrack Obama as their first black American President. This was the time Americans elected a president not based on the colour of his skin but by the content of his character. I could highlight many other people who have had dreams and visions and what they have achieved as a result. However, I would like to challenge you, do you want to go down in history as a person who had a dream and lived to fulfill it? Let's start this journey together and capture our dream through personal visioning.

It is for this reason that I am convinced that we all need to go through a process of personal visioning. It would be great to do this as an individual but it will have a better impact if you do it with your spouse, your best friend (if you are married and your spouse is not your best friend then that is very sad), or even your buddies. I appreciate that some of us have possibly carried out the activities highlighted in this notebook at different times in their lives but not necessarily documented the results - I challenge you to note these activities in a sequential manner and if possible with the help of a friend. You will be amazed at the results and how this will change your life.

Recently, I have formed the habit of reading books with a pen or pencil in hand. I make notes, underline or even circle words and sentences that catch my attention. Most people I know would disagree with me on this because they would like to lend their books to others or maybe the book is even borrowed. However, this is one notebook that you cannot share with someone else. It is a notebook that will be of no benefit to you if you read it without a pen or pencil in hand. I would therefore suggest that if you do not intend to read it with a pen and pencil, give it away or return it to your bookshelf. It is NOT worth your time.

Lastly, this is a notebook and not a 'reading book'. It is about you and not about the content. The purpose of this notebook is to help you look at yourself, discover yourself and discover what God wants of you, and finally fulfill your dream. It is one notebook you might use more than once or even need to buy a second copy of a few years down the line. I encourage you to do so. Do this every three to four years. It will help you to re-examine at your life and review your dream. Something could have changed that requires you to review where you are headed. A dream not fulfilled is but just a dream. If you can, please review the contents of this notebook and your comments at least once in your lifetime. You will benefit from some of the things you documented and your life will have been shaped.

Always remember there are only two kinds of people in this world – the

realists and the dreamers.

The realists know where they're going. The dreamers have already been

there

Robert Orben

Former Presidential Speechwriter

I have divided this notebook into seasons instead of chapters (as they are normally referred to). My thinking is that the different phases in this notebook are actually seasons that we need to go through. Please therefore bear with my line of thought and enjoy the seasons while at it. In each season, I will share some information on the topic and then I will request you to think through some of the information we will have shared in the season. Jot down your reactions in the space provided. The impact of this notebook will not come from you reading it but from your responses and action points. There is a section that will be only helpful if you are going through the book with someone else as it helps you dig deeper together. I therefore encourage you to go through this book with a close or trusted friend.

There are six seasons that in my view can help you draw a personal vision and therefore capture your dream. In Season One; we start by asking ourselves, what is a vision? After we have appreciated what a vision is, in Season Two we look at the gifts and talents, their source and what they are for. After appreciating our gifts and talents, we will then look at values and how they affect our life in Season Three. At this point, I believe we will be ready to move to Season Four which looks at our strengths and weaknesses and how to improve or eliminate them accordingly. Once we know all this about ourselves, we need to take specific actions. This takes us to Season Five which introduces setting personal goals. We will look at some of the important things to bear in mind when setting goals and how to set goals for life. Please remember that we are doing this in order to capture our dream. We cannot afford to lose sight of the reason we are doing this exercise. Finally, in Season Six, we come up with a way of monitoring our progress so that what we have documented is not in vain. I propose some actions I believe would help you keep track of your dream and then turn it into a reality.

I hope you will enjoy the journey through the seasons of discovering yourself and doing something about your discoveries. Come on. Let's capture our dream through personal visioning together.

Season One

Vision

"Where there is no vision people perish" KJV
"Where there is no vision, the people are
uncontrolled..." BBE
Proverbs 29:18

IN THIS FIRST SEASON, WE will talk about what a vision is, its importance and how we can come up with a vision.

How can we define a vision? Vision is about sight. It is about seeing. When I can see where I am going, I will go there with confidence. I want to believe that sight makes me more confident in my daily walk and that explains why I struggle to walk in the dark. A vision starts from a dream and therefore it is about a dream. A vision is about converting your dream into reality. Do not be scared of dreaming. One of my friends always reminds me that dreams are free of charge. Therefore please dream.

Bill Hybel describes a vision as a picture of the future that produces passion.[4] I like that. There are three things that I would like to explore from this description of a vision. The first one is the **picture**. Pictures tend to illustrate things better and that is why in the lower grades in school, teachers use pictures more than words. We remember things better if they are illustrated using pictures. A vision is a picture. Take a minute and draw a picture of your dream. Use a few words to do that. It could be about where you want to be in your career life, family life, spiritual life or even life in general.

Career Dream _____

_____

Family Dream _____

_____

Spiritual Dream _____

_____

My Dream _____

_____

Secondly, a vision is NOT only a picture but a picture of the **future**. This picture illustrates the future. The picture is painted or coloured to reflect how the future will look like. Imagine a painter painting me ten or twenty years from today. He would probably paint me without hair because from the look on my forehead, he thinks I will have lost all my hair by then. He can also paint my face with a few wrinkles, my body frame a bit fatter and my back slightly bent. This painting will be portraying his thoughts of what I will look like in the future. This painting or picture is an illustration of me in the future. However, I might not be able to change much about the hairline on my head but I can change the fact that I will look fatter with a bent back. I can start working on my physique so that I have a body frame and a back that I will be proud of in the future. I can use my today to create my tomorrow and the future I want. I can make the picture look the way I would like it to look. The picture of the future helps me visualize the future and start acting today to improve the future. How does your future look today? Is your life muddled up in confusion and darkness? If you were to illustrate your future, how would it look? Is there anything you would like to change in that picture? The opportunity to change that picture remains with you. Create the picture of the future that you desire.

Thirdly and lastly, a vision is a picture of the future that produces **passion**. Curt Rosengren, an author and passion catalyst, defines passion as the energy that comes from bringing more of you into what you do. Simply put, it's being who you are and doing what comes naturally. It comes from being in alignment with what comes naturally.[5] Rosengren continues to explain that passion is about what you enjoy doing. What do you enjoy doing? What excites you immediately you start doing it? What produces energy in you immediately you think of doing it? What makes you come alive? When I look at the picture of the future, I should be full of energy to get started. That picture should produce some amazing energy that gets me started and that drives me toward that picture. Remember that passion is about what comes naturally. The picture of the future should not be something I struggle to do but something that I am excited about and I cannot wait to do. When a picture of the future is made up of that, then your vision makes sense. This picture of the future should ignite the fire within me to do what must be done for this dream to come true. This picture will then produce a passion in me to pursue my dream. Does your dream produce passion? Please ensure that your dream brings life to you. Ask yourself, what comes naturally? Write it out.

_____

_____

A vision is a picture of the future that produces passion. This passion should drive me. This passion should drive us. However, until that picture of the future produces passion then that picture is NOT good enough. It is NOT worth being called a vision. Get another vision. Get another picture of the future, one that makes you long to wake up tomorrow morning.

IMPORTANCE OF A VISION

When you are thinking of a vision and a personal vision for that matter, it must point you to the future and give you the direction for the future. A vision can NEVER be about today. It must be where you want to be in the future; tomorrow.

Secondly, a vision gives us reason to live with enthusiasm. What a vision stirs in any of us is excitement. A vision should make anyone happy. Ask any person who is married or who has been married at one time in their life (and had a wedding ceremony) and they will tell you what the dream of their wedding day did to them. When I asked my wife to marry me, the thought of the wedding day excited me. I started by painting (in my mind) a picture of how the wedding day would look. I would have narrated it to an artist and they would have drawn it with ease because of the details I would have given them. I am sure any bride can do an even better job painting a mental picture of her wedding day. The excitement of that day made me smile all the time. No wonder people say that you can know a man or woman in love. They are always smiling to themselves. The enthusiasm in my life at that time was because of the vision of our wedding day, my picture of that future day. A vision MUST produce enthusiasm and excitement otherwise it is not worth having.

What a vision stirs in any of us is excitement.

Thirdly, a vision simplifies decision-making. In life I have had to make decisions on a daily basis and at times on an hourly basis. When we have a vision, decision-making is simplified. One of my values is honesty. What this means is that some things are a NO! NO! This does not mean that I do not fall, I do, but I get up and keep walking. Let me not digress. Therefore, if I am caught in a situation where a policeman or government official demands a bribe from me so that he can provide me with my rightful service, I say no. Why? It is very clear in my mind what I want and where I want to be. The fact that this is very clear in my mind makes decision-making very easy for me. Many times I have had to live with the consequences of that particular decision. I remember one day I was arrested in Nairobi city centre for double parking while waiting for a parking slot to become available. (This is a common practice as it is difficult to get parking in the city during the day). The traffic policemen asked me whether I wanted to "reason" with him and find a way out of my situation. I said no and as a result spent the next six hours in a police station having a police bond written out. That was after coughing up the money to pay for the bond. I spent another eight hours in court the following day only to be fined an amount less than the bond I had paid. Can you imagine that it took a policeman at the station six hours to write out the charge sheet which ran only six lines? Those were the consequences of having a vision and keeping it (but I have never regretted that). If I had "reasoned" with the police officer as he had proposed, it would have taken me less than five minutes to conclude the issue and maybe a third of the amount paid as fine in court.

One of my best friends had a girlfriend who was also studying for her Master's degree while he was in graduate school. She wanted to enroll in a PhD program in Europe immediately after. My friend on the other hand wanted to go and work with students and professionals in colleges and universities after completing his studies besides taking up a job. Initially, my friend struggled with these thoughts and their relationship. However, one morning, he looked at his vision and realized that unless his vision in life was going to change, their relationship was bound to suffer. Later, both of them realized that their life visions were different and the relationship eventually ended. Both have since pursued their dreams and, to the best of my knowledge, are both happy doing want they enjoy and pursuing their individual visions. What is my point? Once they looked at the picture of their future, it was easier for them to reach a decision on their relationship. They realized that this relationship could not work for them. Please note that I am not implying that this was without hurt but merely that it was simpler due to the fact that they had a clear vision of their future.

Lastly, a vision always entails progress. A vision is never satisfied with status quo. My dream house is a large four bed-roomed house with a TV room, study room (with a wall to wall bookshelf), kitchen opening to the dining room, a basketball court at the front yard next to the grass lawn, and a swimming pool not to mention the kitchen garden in the backyard and a BMW 4*4 Station wagon parked at the front yard. Where am I today? I am living in a four bed-roomed house with a front grass lawn (though not manicured) and driving a 1,000 c.c. litre engine car. This means that I cannot be satisfied with the status quo when I wake up and remember my grand picture and realize that I am far from achieving it. A vision makes us desire the picture of the future and then do what it takes to get there. You can be sure I am working very hard to get there. If a vision does not elicit that desire, then it is time to change it.

A SPIRITUAL BASED VISION

The International Christian Centre Pastoral teaching team when running a series on 'a vision to die for' in 2010, summarized a vision as follows. "A God-Inspired vision is God-imparted, change-oriented, action-packed, faith-based and realistic".

If you are an individual who loves and worships God, you need a vision that is God-imparted. It should be derived from God's word and based on your faith. Your vision needs to reflect your faith. It needs to be rooted in God's word. Secondly, your vision needs to be change-oriented. It needs to be a vision that not only changes you but one that changes people around your environment. Your vision needs to make you a people-changer. It should enable you turn around people's hearts. This should not be by words only but by actions mainly. People should desire to have you around because you cause change. Thirdly, your vision should be realistic. It should be a vision that is built on what is happening on earth. It should not be a vision that looks at spiritual issues to the point of forgetting that we are still on earth. As spiritual people, we at times tend to lose touch with the world. You need a vision that is in touch with reality and one that is in touch with what is happening around the world today. I cannot belabour the point about having a vision. If you are a Christian, a vision, begins with God's priority, includes others, is tangible, easily communicated, and has eternal value or significance.

GETTING STARTED

One, you can have more than one vision for your life. You can have a career vision, a family vision, a spiritual vision, a personal vision etc.

Two, you need to have one (all-encompassing) vision that directs your entire life.

Third, you need to convert your vision into a statement.

Let me share my own personal example: I believe that God created me to influence people around me in everything that I do. I therefore live to influence people. In my work place, I will always ask myself, I am influencing anyone at the moment. I do the same in my social life, when I volunteer to help out in any activity in church, or even in our children's school. Secondly, my objective is not to influence crowds. I believe if I can influence one person at a time, and do it well; the impact will be greater because they can also do the same thereafter and the chain will keep going on and on. That does not mean that influencing crowds is wrong or not tenable. I just believe in influencing one person at a time. From this, I derived my vision statement that states as follows: "Positively influencing one person as a time". This vision guides me. It directs my dreams, my thoughts, my actions, my career choices, my commitments etc. When I am doing something, I will normally ask myself, is this action influencing someone or is it about me? If it is about me, I drop it and look for something else to do.

Let me share a few personal vision statements that I came across on a website known as www.humanresources.about.com which I think will shed some light on what vision statements are all about. A guest by the name Benson Baguma says that his personal vision is, "To impact the lives of others through godliness in mine". Another guest Eic Marudo says that his life vision is to be a "responsible father, husband, son, big brother to my family. Upholding love, simple life and obey our God at all times." Guest Afisunlu Opeyemi's dream is, "I look to the future to be a Network Specialist and an IT consultant and a loving father." Guest V Duffey from Australia says that my vision is, "I want to make a difference with what I do, be good at it and have a positive influence on those around me." Guest Carrol who is a life coach says that her personal vision is, "I am the spark that lights the fire. I aim to make a difference in someone's life, every day, in any way." Guest Tom San's personal vision makes me smile; he says, "My journey in life is about becoming a positive influence, where people feel better for having met me." What you realize about all this statements is that they are personal. They are descriptive of the owners. Secondly, they describe what the person wants to achieve in life. A vision must be personal and it must state what you desire to achieve. It could be to influence others, be responsible, or even make a difference somewhere. A vision is continuous and in the future. A vision is not about the past or today but about the future and what you will do about it.

THINKING THROUGH

Before we proceed from this point, I would like you to do something about what we have been talking about. Remember my opening statement, that this is not a 'reading book' but a 'notebook'. Let's jot down some things that we have observed. This will help us put to use the information that I have shared above and the same will be of use to you.

1. What are your thoughts from this season and why?

    _____

    _____

    _____

    _____

2. What was the most outstanding element of a vision to you?

    _____

    _____

    _____

    _____

3. What did you dream you would become when you grew up? Draw a picture of that dream. Use words if you are not good in drawing.

    _____

    _____

_____

_____

4. Has your dream come true or not? If not, why? If yes, how?

_____

_____

_____

_____

5. How would you describe a vision? (Avoid getting caught-up discussing my description of a vision). What is your description?

_____

_____

_____

_____

6. Why else (besides those stated in Season I) do you think a vision is important?

_____

_____

_____

_____

DIGGING DEEPER TOGETHER

I would like us to explore the thought deeper and do it together so that we can achieve some results. Rosengren, in his book "The occupational adventure guide", encourages people to look at themselves and then ask, "What do I love doing?" This helps to bring out the passion in them and I dare to add, their vision. After that he says, please find out why you love doing what you love doing and keep doing that for the next five responses you give. I also suggest that you ask yourself, what have I always dreamt of being or doing? Now ask yourself, why?

Let me share my own example. I love to talk to people about why they hold certain thoughts. Why? I get to know the thoughts of that person. Why? It helps me to appreciate the person more. Why? I get to understand what their values are. Why? They get to explain what influences their values. Why? I get to understand the person and maybe influence their opinion by giving them my thoughts on the issue. My vision is positively influencing one person at a time. By digging deeper into what I love doing, I realized that the main reason why I love talking to people is because I would like to influence them. I therefore talk to people about their thoughts simply because I hope to understand them and then influence their thoughts.

What is one of my many dreams? I have always dreamt of owning a retreat centre which has a garden that provides food for the retreat centre. Why? I have always wanted to create a place that provides fun and relaxation for people at a minimal cost. Why? This would be able to give me a flexible working schedule. Why? With a flexible working schedule, I can dedicate some of my time to working with people and not expecting them to pay me for that time I spend with them. Why? I will be able to impact knowledge and values that I believe are lacking in the world today. Why? I will influence the person I am dealing with and in return they will influence someone else. Why? The impact is greater and deeper.

Now do this for yourselves. If you do this with someone else, they can help you get to the bottom of your reason.

1. Why do I love doing what I do?

   _____

   _____

   _____

   _____

2. Why?

_____

_____

3. Why?

_____

_____

…

4. What have I dreamt of doing?

_____

_____

_____

_____

5. Why?

_____

_____

6. Why?

_____

_____

…Now with all that you jotted down above, write out your first draft of a vision below. Incorporate your dream for your career/business, family, spiritual life and even life in general.

My vision is……..

_____

_____

_____

_____

Convert this long paragraph into a single statement or sentence of between 8 and 12 words. Remember the statement needs to be personal, descriptive of you and about the future. You can review the examples of personal visions shared earlier if it will help you formulate yours.

My vision statement is……

_____

_____

Do not be scared of jotting something down. It does not have to be perfect at this point. Just do it. Remember, if you move from this point without writing your vision, you will have missed the point of this notebook. You might as well drop this notebook and move on with your life as though you'd never bought it.

Jot something down and you can come back and amend it as we go on. Use a pencil if you must, so that you can erase it later. But make sure you write it down.

Season Two

Stewardship

Do more than belong; participate. Do more than care;
help. Do more than believe; practice. Do more than be
fair: be kind. Do more than forgive; forget. *Do more than
dream; work.* (Italics mine)
William Arthur War
American, Author and Pastor (1921 – 1994)

LET'S TAKE A STEP BACK and remind ourselves where we started.
A vision is a picture of the future that produces passion. A vision
is about sight. A vision is about tomorrow. The picture helps
us remain focused and passion is about what comes naturally.
However, a vision is achieved through gifts and talents.

A gift or talent is what God has given you. One may just
be gifted in creating life wherever they go. We have this friend
who is such a party maker. Tony just needs to come into a room
and it does not matter what was going on, the room will come
to life. Tony has all manner of stories and lessons to share from
his life. If the situation is solemn, he will walk with you and
make everyone reflect on the situation at hand; be it dealing with
death, sickness, you name it. If the situation is joyful, he will get
everyone laughing. By the time you are done with Tony, you are
refreshed despite your circumstance. Tony has taken advantage
of his talent and worked with the youth in Nairobi for over ten
years. Young people love stories especially those they can identify
with. That is what Tony is able to do. He turned his gift into a
career and for ten years, he influenced the youth in Nairobi. He
shared his life, made the young people laugh, challenged their
lives and finally helped them make the right choices.

Each of us has a gift or talent. The question is therefore, have you identified your gift or talent? If you have, how are you using it? Remember that you will still be accountable for your gift whether you use it or not. Talents do not have to be tangible or visible or even something you can give out. It could be a skill. Look at Tony, his talent is being a sanguine (cheerful and a story teller) and look at how he has used it. I know of this other lady who loves children. She enjoys playing with children, feeding them and just holding them. She is a blessing to parents by being available to step in and take care of children during holidays or when a family does not have a home helper or even during church functions. The last time my wife spoke to her, she was thinking of using this gift to make a living while helping out at the same time. This is not just about things that you can see or use, it could just be about a skill that you have. A doctor can choose to give up a certain number of hours every month to serve people who cannot afford to pay for medical services. A carpenter can take a young man straight from school as an apprentice in his shop and train him at no cost. It all depends on your vision. Depending on what you have always dreamt of, you can use that gift and talents within you to achieve that vision. Gifts and talents can be used to achieve visions while visions are achieved through gifts and talents.

A steward is someone who is in charge of something. When we are stewards, we are taking care of something we are holding for someone. When we use it, we must remember that it belongs to someone else. A caretaker of a building is a steward. He or she takes care of the building on behalf of the owner. Most of the time, the owner is not there and if he or she is, is not involved in the day-to-day running of the building. The caretaker makes sure all the tenants have what they need by ensuring that the building is repaired as the need arises and all the tenants are sharing the premises as expected of them. The caretaker has instructions from the owner and serves the tenants according to their needs. It does not matter how long the caretaker serves, the building will not become his or hers unless ownership changes. People may think that the caretaker is the owner because of how he or she may behave but that does not make them the owner. This is the same with our gifts and talents. They will never be ours despite the fact that they look like they belong to us.

Moreover, it is required of stewards that one is found trustworthy.

1 Cor 4:2 NASB

Now it is required that those who have been given a trust must prove

faithful

1 Cor 4:2 NIV

Gifts are things given to us by someone. We hardly get the chance to choose a gift. The giver just hands it to us and we accept it. A talent is not any different. However, we tend to identify talents with the things God has put in us and those that we can use. Many times we have forgotten that these talents and gifts were given to us and we had no part in them being given to us. We discovered these gifts as we grew up or they were identified in us by other people. Just like the caretaker, these gifts and talents are to be used to serve other people NOT necessarily ourselves. We are merely caretakers and stewards of these gifts.

Gifts and talents are not meant for the user but for the receiver. Why do I say that? When we let gifts and talents be for our own use, we only benefit ourselves. We therefore become proud and selfish. When we use gifts and talents to benefit others, we influence them, we change their situations and make them better and different people. God gave us those gifts and talents so that we can produce and reproduce ourselves.

"A story is told of a King who gave out his wealth to three of his servants to manage. To the first one, he gave ten portions, to the second he gave five portions and to the third he gave one portion. The first and the second servants reproduced ten and five more portions respectively. Unfortunately, the third servant did not reproduce their portion as they held their portion and did nothing with it. A time came for the King to evaluate his servants' performance. The King commended the first and the second servants for doing a great job but condemned the third servant for holding on to and doing nothing with his portion. His reasoning was that the servant should at have least invested the portion of the wealth given to him so that his master could profit from it. The King then ordered that the one portion he had given the third servant be taken away and given to the first servant.[6]"

We can learn three lessons from this story. The first lesson is that God gives gifts according to one's **ability**. Our abilities are not the same. God did not create all of us the same. He knows that some of us can be political leaders while others can be administrators. The gift God gives me is according to my abilities. To one servant, the King gave ten portions of his wealth, to another five portions of his wealth and to another only one portion. The king knew the ability of each servant. Unfortunately the servant who was given one portion proved the King right by doing nothing with his portion.

The second lesson is that God expects us to **use** our gift according to our ability. When the first servant brought ten more portions, the King commended him. When the second servant brought five more portions of wealth, the King commend him also. Why did the King do so? It was because they had used their gifts according to their abilities and that is all that the King expected. God does not expect the teacher to perform like a political leader. The teacher is meant to teach and ensure that they impart knowledge while teaching. A political leader is meant to give direction, and ensure that the resources placed under him or her are well managed. The teacher cannot be punished or condemned for not ensuring that the political region where he or she teaches has water but he or she will be condemned for not teaching and training the students in their class.

The third lesson we can learn is that we must **reproduce** our gifts. Although God has given us gifts, it will not be enough for us to have the same gifts at the end of time. We need to reproduce them. The first and second servants reproduced the portion of wealth that had been given to them. The third servant was condemned for not reproducing it. All he did he was keep what had been given to him. The King not only condemned him but also took away the portion of wealth given to him and had it given to the first servant who had reproduced his. What God has given us needs to be reproduced otherwise we will be like the third servant whom the King condemned. Our gifts are not ours to keep to make ourselves proud and selfish. Our gifts are for reproducing. Let us be good caretakers who ensure that the owner of the building gets the rental income due because the building is well kept and fully occupied.

God has given gifts to each of you from his great variety of spiritual gifts.
Manage them well so that God's generosity can flow through you.
1 Peter 4:10 NLT

Let me conclude this season with another story.

"The Late Spencer Penrose, whose brother was a major political leader in Philadelphia in the late nineteenth century, was considered the "black sheep" of the family. He chose to live in the West, instead of the East. In 1891, fresh out of Harvard, he made his way to Colorado Springs. Not long after his move, he wired his brother for $1,500.00 so that he might go into a mining venture. His brother telegraphed him 150.00 instead – enough for train fare home - and warned him against the deal.

Years later, Spencer returned to Philadelphia and handed his brother $75,000.00 in gold coins - payment, he said for his "investment" in his mining operation. His brother was stunned. He had qualms about accepting the money, however, and reminded his brother that he had advised against the venture and had only given him $150.00. "That" replied Spencer, "is why I'm only giving you $75,000.00. If you had sent me the full $1,500.00 I requested, I would be giving you $750,000.00."

Nothing invested, nothing gained. Every harvest requires an initial seed. Be generous in your seed sowing. Plant in good ground and you can anticipate a good harvest. That's the secret of good stewardship."[7]

We can learn two more lessons from Spencer's life.

One, that as a good steward, it is my responsibility to remain faithful. Spencer's brother did not expect any return from the train fare turned "investment", but Spencer choose to still give him his returns.

Two, nothing invested, nothing gained. God has given us a gift or talent but it is up to us to invest it. Will we do like the servant with ten portions of wealth or the one who had one portion of wealth? The choice is ours. We can start whining about how our gift is inferior, or how our gift is not like Tom's or Mary's. However, the bottom line is this: what will we do with our gift or talent? Will we reproduce it or sit on it? Let's make the wise and right choice.

GETTING STARTED

What are my gifts and talents? Remember, I recommended that you do this with your spouse, friend or buddies. They know you and they will speak into your life and especially during this season.

1. What are your thoughts from this season and why?

   _____

   _____

   _____

   _____

2. Note down some of the gifts and talents you believe you have. (This is what you think). It is not yet time to ask other people what they think of you. (I have a gifting of being able to get things organized, what about you?)

   _____

   _____

   _____

   _____

DIGGING DEEPER TOGETHER

3. Now, ask your team mates (in this case spouse, best friend or buddy); what are some of the gifts and talents they see in you? Jot them down. If they are different from what you had written, ask them why and let them explain.

    _____

    _____

    _____

    _____

4. How can you use these gifts and talents? (One of my gifts is organizational skills. How can I use it? I can use it to coordinate events, activities, or functions.) List yours here. Your team mates can help where possible.

    _____

    _____

    _____

    _____

5. What are some of the challenges that you have encountered while trying to use your gifts and talents? (E.g. If I wanted to work as an administrator, I might be unable to get a job due to my current qualifications and experience.)

    _____

    _____

    _____

    _____

6. How can you manage or reduce the gap created by the challenges you are having while trying to use your gifts and talents? (To overcome the challenge of academic qualification,

I may need to take a course in organizational management or leadership skill to enhance my skills)

_____

_____

_____

_____

7. How does this tie in with your vision? Start by jotting down your vision below and then try and connect you gifting to your vision. (My vision is "positively influencing people one at a time." How can I use my organizational skill to influence people? I start by organizing activities even if they are social or just by being part of them. I will then identify one person in the group on whom I can impart knowledge. With time, I influence their life in different ways.)

My vision is …

_____

_____

It connects to my gifts in this way...

_____

_____

8. Do you need to re-align your vision in view of your gifts and talents? Please feel free to do so. That is the purpose of this notebook. It is meant to help you achieve your desires.

_____

_____

_____

_____

Season Three

Values

A value is a conviction that guides any individual or organization.
International Christian Centre Pastoral Team (2010)
Lasting change is a series of compromises. And compromise is all right, as long as your values don't change.
Jane Goodall
British Anthropologist & UN Peace Messenger

LET'S REVIEW WHAT WE HAVE discussed in the last two seasons. A vision is a picture of the future that produces passion. Take a minute and read through your draft vision statement.

My vision is ....

_____

_____

A vision is achieved through gifts and talents. We do not choose our God-given gifts and talents, but we are responsible for them. We need to be faithful stewards of the gifts and talents God has given us.

Values are things that are important, useful, and of worth to us. Values are the things that matter to any individual, family, and any kind of organization. When Coca Cola Company says that, "We value quality", what is it saying? It goes further to say, "What we do, we do it well."[8] It values quality by doing what it does well. Unilever PLC, manufacturer of Omo washing powder,

Blue-band margarine, and many other household products has an interesting and powerful value that is recorded as follows; "Always working with integrity". It goes further to explain what it mean through the following statement: "We conduct our operations with integrity and with respect for the many people, organizations and environments our business touches".[9] That tells you why Coca Cola values quality and Unilever, integrity. For those of us who have ever drank a soda bottled by Coca Cola or a product produced by Unilever, we know that they believe in their values and live up to them. I hope you have noted that these values describe what these two companies believe in and exist for.

The pastoral team of International Christian Centre when teaching the series on a "vision to die for"[10] in 2010, noted that a value is a conviction that guides any individual or organization. Values therefore guide any vision that an individual or organization adopts. As an individual or organization, you can have very many values that guide your life. These are your convictions. However, you need to name the ones that are deal-breakers in your life. These you cannot forgive yourself (not literally though) if you broke them. That is, if broken, your life would feel empty.

Organizations call these values, Core Values or Principles. They are the core and all the activities of the organization revolve around them. A. Malphurs states that core values explain who one is (one's identity) and they form the basis for the vision and mission of a ministry.[11] The State of Iowa uses the words 'guiding principles' and says that they represent an organization's attitude, influence how the organization is managed, how decisions are made and products and services provided. They continue to say that core values should express fundamental belief, the conditions that people work in and the basis for the decisions about the kind of structures, systems and skills required to achieve the vision.[12] A. Malphurs goes further and introduces another aspect of core values which I feel compelled to also share with you. He says that core values should dictate personal involvement, communicate what is important, embrace good change, influence overall behaviours and also inspire people to action.[13] I need to stop here in regard to strategic planning for organizations, another of my pet subjects.

I would like to borrow a few thoughts from these descriptions of core values by Malphurs and the State of Iowa. Core values should influence how we make decisions as the decisions we make relate to our overall behaviour. Core values are about **influence** (now you know where my vision statement came from). When I think of influence, I think of change. When I influence someone, they change from one thing to another, from one behaviour to another. However, influence should not be just about change BUT positive change. In my opinion, a core value MUST positively influence us; otherwise it is not core to me. The core value that each individual adopts must generate positive change. What are some values that come to mind that you would like to adapt?

_____

_____

Secondly, core values should **express** something. Core values need to express one's heart. They need to express one's beliefs and convictions. If they do not, then they are not good core values. What do the values you have thought express?

_____

_____

Thirdly, core values need to **communicate** what is important to you. Is honesty important to you? Then it needs to be core for you. Ask yourself, what does my core value communicate?

Lastly, core values must **inspire**. The core values need to give purpose to the individual. It needs to be the reason why the person lives and why their vision exists. What do you live for? Why do you exist?

_____

_____

"A story is told of a young man, the 11th son in a family of 12 boys. He was born to the second wife of his father. His ten step-brothers decided to sell him to trade merchants because they felt their father loved him more than the rest of them. They had reason to believe so as their father had bought him the most beautiful coat anyone could own in their time. Before his step-brothers sold him, they thought of killing him but the eldest of them all pleaded with them not to. This young man was taken to a foreign country by the merchants who sold him to a government official as a house servant. Unfortunately, the wife of the government official noticed that this young man was good looking and tried to seduce him. When her persuasion failed she framed the young man for attempting to rape her and the government official got the young man thrown into prison. Being sold to a foreign land was not bad enough; he was now in prison for doing the right thing. While in prison, he was so humble and hardworking that the prison warden made him the chief prisoner. What a promotion. Chief prisoner? Another interesting thing happened while he was in prison. Anyone who had a dream and did not know what it meant got it interpreted by the chief prisoner. Eventually, the King also had a dream and one of his servants told him of this young man in prison who once interpreted his dream. The King then called for the chief prisoner who then interpreted his dream. The King was so impressed that he made the chief prisoner his Prime Minister. What a turn of events."[14]

What are some values that I think this young man had? He had perseverance, integrity, trustworthiness, forgiveness, humility among many other values. These are good values to hold. The young man lived the way he did because of these values. They guided his life. Do your values guide your life? Jane Goodall, a British anthropologist and UN peace messenger said, "Lasting change is a series of compromises. And compromise is all right, as long as your values don't change." Remember you can change many other things but values are permanent. They do not change unless the conviction changes.

The International Christian Centre "vision to die for" series[15] listed the following six components for value based living. Value based living:

1. Gives focus and direction,

2. Increases productivity,

3. Creates unity of purpose,

4. Defines a person,

5. Offers predictability of behaviour and

6. Results in fruitfulness.

The wrong convictions lead to the wrong actions. Consider famous personalities such as Former Presidents Idd Amin Dada of Uganda, Adolf Hitler of Germany, Saddam Hussein of Iraq and many others. These men held convictions which most of us will agree were wrong and in return were a great disservice to their nations and the world at large. A wrong conviction could be due to a wrong belief. A wrong belief could be due to a wrong teaching. We therefore need to ensure that we get the correct teaching and even verify all the teachings we receive. We need to keep checking our convictions because they form our values. If our values are wrong, we will make wrong decisions. We must have the right convictions otherwise we might end up like these men or many others we can name or think of. List the convictions behind the values your listed earlier and think through the conviction. Is this value worth holding?

Value _____

Conviction _____

Value _____

Conviction _____

Value _____

Conviction _____

I will conclude with this statement from the pastoral team of International Christian Centre, "When an individual is value-driven, then the family and the church will be value-driven".

I dare to add my own. If everyone had a vision and core values for their own lives, most organizations would have the right people on their staff and they would operate more efficiently as people would work for organizations with values they can relate to. Do you have values that guide your actions?

GETTING STARTED

1. What are your thoughts from this season and why?

   _____

   _____

   _____

   _____

2. How would you describe a value? (Feel free to use a dictionary)

   _____

   _____

   _____

   _____

3. Why do you think values are important?

   _____

   _____

   _____

   _____

4. What are some values that the organization you work for or have worked for had?

   _____

   _____

   _____

   _____

THINKING THROUGH

5. Which are some values you think would be good to have and why? Write out your earlier list below and add more if need be.

_____

_____

_____

_____

6. Let's write out your vision and gifts/talents below. This will help us to keep going and thinking about them.

My vision statement is...

_____

_____

My gifts/talents are...

_____

_____

7. List some values you would like to adopt.

_____

_____

_____

_____

8. List between 4 and 6 core values aligned to your vision and gifts/talents that you would like to adopt. You can use a word that consolidates some of the values you have listed above.

Against each value, write a few words describing what this value means to you. (Honesty – Being truthful, open and transparent: Godly – Being clean, spiritual, respectful)

_____

_____

_____

_____

9. Do you want to realign or re-word your vision? As you conclude, please feel free to do so.

_____

_____

Season Four

Strengths, Weaknesses and Your Personality

"...People are different from each other... no amount of getting after them is going to change them. Nor is there reason to change them, because the differences are probably good."
David Keirsey, PhD
Author of "Please understand me II"

LET'S START WITH A RECAP of the last three seasons. A vision is a picture of the future that produces passion. Remember to keep that picture at the back of your mind. A vision is achieved through gifts and talents. These gifts and talents are given to us by God and we are simply custodians of them. They do not belong to us. Core values are each person's convictions and they influence others, express beliefs, communicate what is important to us and inspire one's life. Up to this point, we have drafted a vision for our life, we have identified our gifts and talents and we have also come up with between four and six values we want to live for. Please do not get tired of jotting things down. Once again, let's just jot down our vision, gifts and talents, and values.

My vision statement is...

_____

_____

My gifts/talents are…

_____

_____

My core values are … (Between 4 and 6)

_____

_____

_____

_____

_____

Look at the great men in history. The most successful ones have been faulted for one thing or another. In fact the longer one stays in power, the higher the possibility of them getting corrupt. Power corrupts and despite the great strides that one has achieved, when they get corrupted by power, their weakness becomes evident. The current President of Uganda, Yoweri Museveni, made very good strides for Uganda when he took over the country through a coup. Years down the line, Ugandans say he is a dictator and has even gagged the media. President Paul Kagame, of Rwanda is another example. He took over a country that had suffered from genocide and has done amazing and great things. However, according to his opponents, power is getting to his head. Opposition members in Rwanda are being killed or imprisoned. What am I implying? Everyone has weaknesses and strengths. These two great men I have mentioned have achieved what their predecessors were unable to do. They found countries in ruins and people suffering; using their skills and they have brought their countries back on the path to economic recovery. Their strengths are evident but over time, so are their weaknesses.

In life, we tend to address weaknesses more because they are often conspicuous and then we ignore the strengths. When we talk about our personalities and how we can realize our potential, more often than not, we consider how we can eliminate our weaknesses to improve ourselves. I am however convinced that we need is to concentrate on improving our strengths instead of eliminating our weaknesses. When we concentrate on eliminating our weaknesses we spend less time improving on our strengths and in effect weakening our strengths. In the process, we end up with more weaknesses and less strengths because some of the strengths we had have deteriorated and therefore the weaknesses become even more conspicuous. Think of it this way, when you work on your strengths they are elevated and more pronounced and your weaknesses diminish in comparison. Secondly, it takes more energy to eliminate your weaknesses than to improve your strengths.

Strengths are our positives

I have to complete this paint job today.

Strengths are our positives. Strengths are the things that make us shine. When I say that President Kagame's strength is in being an effective leader, what do I mean? President Kagame found a country torn oozing from bloodshed after the 1994 genocide. In the words of Andrew Harding, "In 1994, his rebel army ended Rwanda's genocide. Since then his government has worked to transform a shattered nation into one of Africa's least corrupt, fastest-growing, most competent countries. It is an extraordinary achievement, and most Rwandans are quick to credit their president"[16] That is the positive. President Kagame has been credited with what Rwanda is today. Strengths make everyone around you smile and excited that you are around. Your life and the lives of people around you are good simply because of your presence. Strengths are what everyone desires. When you look at someone else and you admire them or even wish you were like them, it is their strengths that make them desirable.

Weaknesses are our negatives

On the other hand, weaknesses are our negatives. This is normally everyone's undoing. It is why everyone around me wishes me out. It is the thing that makes people wish Muthengi was not here or did not do that. A weakness spoils the party. It can spoil all the gains one has achieved. Weaknesses are traits that we wish we did not have. There is a community in Kenya that is known for having a short fuse. They spark so easily. They lose their tempers and sometime cause devastating damage while at it. I tend to be careful around people of that community. That short fuse is a weakness.

Strengths and Weaknesses are said to have something to do with our personalities. A personality can be defined as "the pattern of collective character, behavioural, temperamental, emotional, and mental traits of a person."[17] It can also be defined as "an individual's characteristic patterns of thought, emotion, and behaviour, together with the psychological mechanisms - hidden or not - behind those patterns" (Funder, 2001, p.2).[18]

Which do I take?

A personality is about one's thoughts and feelings. Some people think while others feel. You will hear someone say that "I think the best thing to do is call off this meeting because we are not making any headway". Another person will then respond by saying "I feel that will not be a good decision, let's keep this going for a few more minutes before giving up". It is the difference in personalities between these two individuals that leads them to either think or feel a certain way.

A personality is also about behaviour. We all behave differently because of our personalities. Some of us are hot-tempered; others are composed, some are outgoing while others are reserved. Why is the issue of temperaments important? In my opinion, understanding one's temperament helps them know their strengths and weaknesses.

I am not a trained psychologist and neither am I a clinical psychiatrist. The issue of temperaments started many centuries ago. In 450BC, Hippocrates came up with four temperaments that are commonly talked about namely: Choleric, Sanguine, Melancholic and Phlegmatic. I took a lot of time several years ago to study a book titled, "Spirit-controlled Temperaments" by Tim LaHaye. I therefore have some idea of the topic and will take you through the four temperaments as described by Dr. LaHaye and hopefully help you identify your temperament. In my very recent research on the internet, I bumped into a website by Dr David Keirsey. Dr Keirsey has approached temperaments differently and has classified them into four categories namely: Guardian, Rational, Idealist and Artisan. Honestly speaking I cannot tie them to the four traditional temperaments, one to one. Dr. Keirsey breaks down the four categories to another sixteen. The traditional way of classifying temperaments can be described as follows:

Traditional Categorization

Sanguine	Choleric
• Self-composed	• Self-composed
• Not given to worry	• Not given to worry
• Liberal	• Persuasive
• Tends to follow rather than lead	• Independent
• Cordial	• Rarely shows embarrassment
• Peaceable	• Tends to lead rather than follow
• Talkative	• Persistent
• Not averse to change	• Insistent
• Adjusts easily	• Decisive
• Tends to prefer informality	• Dynamic
• Aware of surroundings	• Impetuous
• Impetuous	• Impulsive
• Impulsive	• Touchy
• Lacking in perseverance	• Prone to hypocrisy, deceit, pride, and anger
• Lacking in initiative	
• Prone to carelessness, hedonism, flightiness, and lust	

Melancholic	Phlegmatic
• Sensitive	• Peaceful
• Intuitive	• Easy-going
• Self-conscious	• Deliberative
• Easily embarrassed	• Faithful
• Easily hurt	• Reliable
• Introspective	• Relatively unaffected by environment
• Sentimental	
• Moody	• Reserved
• Likes to be alone	• Distant
• Empathetic	• Slow in movement
• Often artistic	• Constant in mood
• Often fussy and perfectionist	• Not prone to worry
• Deep	• Prone to stagnation and sloth
• Prone to depression, avarice, and gluttony	

Table 1[19]

It is rare to find anyone who is a pure sanguine, choleric, melancholic or phlegmatic. Most people will have a combination of two or three temperaments. However, one of these temperaments is dominant. Sanguines and Cholerics are the extroverts while the Melancholics and Phlegmatics are the introverts. The Sanguines are known as the party makers, the Cholerics are the born leaders, the Melancholics are the perfectionists while the Phlegmatics are the easy-going guys. You can do a simple exercise using the above table and tick the statements that best describes you. The box with the most items ticks is your dominant temperament while the second most is your secondary temperament. Do not tick what you would want to be but what you are.

Secondly, depending with the environment, your temperament can change. When I was doing my bachelor's degree, I was a Melancholic – Choleric. My day would start at noon and I was extremely moody. I was also a perfectionist holding on to items for sentimental attachments. Years later after meeting a friend who mentored me as a young Christian and who was a very strong Choleric, I shifted and become a stronger Choleric and less Melancholic. My various responsibilities in the office, at home and in church have not made it any better and currently I am a Choleric – Melancholic. I am more decisive, preferring to lead than follow.

Dr.Keirsey's four classifications can be described as below:

Keirsey's Temperaments

Guardian	Rational
• Guardians pride themselves on being dependable, helpful, and hard-working. • Guardians make loyal mates, responsible parents, and stabilizing leaders. • Guardians tend to be dutiful, cautious, humble, and focused on credentials and traditions. • Guardians are concerned citizens who trust authority, join groups, seek security, prize gratitude, and dream of meting out justice.	• Rationals tend to be pragmatic, skeptical, self-contained, and focused on problem-solving and systems analysis. • Rationals pride themselves on being ingenious, independent, and strong willed. • Rationals make reasonable mates, individualizing parents, and strategic leaders. • Rationals are even-tempered, they trust logic, yearn for achievement, seek knowledge, prize technology, and dream of understanding how the world works.
Administrators • Inspectors e.g. Queen Elizabeth II • Supervisors e.g. George Washington **Conservators** • Protectors e.g. Mother Theresa • Providers e.g. J C Penney	**Engineers** • Architects e.g. Albert Einstein • Inventors e.g. Walt Disney **Coordinators** • Masterminds e.g. Isaac Newton • Field marshals e.g. Hillary Clinton

Idealist	Artisan
• Idealists are enthusiastic, they trust their intuition, yearn for romance, seek their true self, prize meaningful relationships, and dream of attaining wisdom. • Idealists pride themselves on being loving, kind-hearted, and authentic. • Idealists tend to be giving, trusting, spiritual, and they are focused on personal journeys and human potentials. • Idealists make intense mates, nurturing parents, and inspirational leaders.	• Artisans tend to be fun-loving, optimistic, realistic, and focused on the here and now • Artisans pride themselves on being unconventional, bold, and spontaneous. • Artisans make playful mates, creative parents, and troubleshooting leaders. • Artisans are excitable, trust their impulses, want to make a splash, seek stimulation, prize freedom, and dream of mastering action skills.

Advocates	Entertainers
• Healers e.g. Princess Diana	• Composers e.g. Steven Spielberg
• Champions e.g. Charles Dickens	• Performers e.g. Ronald Reagan
Mentors	**Operators**
• Counselors e.g. Mohandas Gandhi	• Crafters e.g. Michael Jordan
• Teachers e.g. Oprah Winfrey	• Promoters e.g. Winston Churchill

Table 2[20]

Dr. Keirsey's temperaments are structured differently. Dr. Keirsey divides his categories into four namely; Guardians, Rationals, Idealists and Artisans. He then goes deeper and divides each category into two. For example, the Guardians are either Administrators or Conservators. The Administrators can either be Inspectors or supervisors while the Conservators can either be protectors or Teachers. By reading through the four categories you can easily identify where you are. However, you would have to take the test on Dr. Keirsey's website to know which of the four sub-categories you fall under.

I would recommend that you get onto the internet and do a personality test immediately if you have not already done one. I would strongly recommend the one by Dr. Keirsey.

GETTING STARTED

What are your thoughts from this season and why?

_____

_____

_____

THINKING THROUGH

Identify your strengths. (How can you work to improve your strengths while reducing your weaknesses unless you know them?)

A personality test is a good place to start. List your strengths and weaknesses.

Strengths according to me

1. _____
2. _____
3. _____
4. _____
5. _____

Weaknesses according to me

1. _____
2. _____
3. _____
4. _____
5. _____

DIGGING DEEPER TOGETHER

Let's take this to another level. Remember we are doing this whole exercise with our spouse, friends or even buddies. Ask them to tell you some of the strengths and weaknesses they see in you.

Strengths according to others

1. _____
2. _____
3. _____
4. _____
5. _____

Weaknesses according to others

1. _____

2. _____

3. _____

4. _____

5. _____

We now know our strengths and weaknesses. If we leave it at that, this exercise will be in vain. We need to ask ourselves, what next? We therefore need an action plan in regard to these many strengths and weaknesses. However, I would suggest that you do not work on all of them at the same time. Start with two strengths and two weaknesses. Pick your top two strengths and bottom two weaknesses in regard to impact and start with those. It will be easier to improve the strengths that standout most. Similarly, it will be easier to address the weaknesses that have the least negative impact in your life. Once you have done a good job on these ones then you can move on.

Strength I need to improve

1. _____

Action _____

2. _____

Action _____

Weakness I need to watch

1. _____

Action _____

2. _____

Action _____

Season Five

Goal Setting

The greater danger for most of us lies not in setting our
aim too high and falling short; but in setting our aim too
low, and achieving our mark.
Michelangelo
Italian Renaissance Painter, Sculptor, Architect, Poet &
Engineer

A RECAP OF THE PREVIOUS seasons helps us see where we are
coming from and what we have achieved. A vision is a picture
of the future that produces passion. We cannot afford to lose
site of the picture that originated from our dream. A vision is
achieved through gifts and talents. Gifts and talents are not ours
to keep but to give out. Core values stem from our convictions.
They influence others, express beliefs, communicate what is
important to us and inspire one's life. Core values are what drive
us. Every individual has strengths and weaknesses. Strengths are
our positive characteristics while weaknesses are our negative
characteristics. Our personalities are built around these. Let's
keep the seasons updated.

My vision statement is…

_____

_____

My gifts/talents are…

_____

My core values are ... (Between 4 and 6)

_____

_____

_____

_____

_____

My Strengths ...

_____

_____

_____

_____

My Weaknesses ...

_____

_____

_____

_____

A goal is an objective or a target that one sets for themselves. After we identify our vision, we need to set a goal. Goal-setting is a powerful process for thinking about your ideal future, and for motivating yourself to turn this vision of the future into reality.[21] When a goal is clearly set, one is able to walk towards it with certainty. A clearly-defined goal gives a person the motivation to keep going and then turn a vision into reality. Goal- setting leads to success.

Goals need to be SMART. A goal needs to be **specific**. My vision is to positively influence one person at a time. I have chosen that I want to influence someone. Secondly, I will do it, one person at a time. That is very specific. A goal needs to be **measurable.** When a goal is measurable, then it means you can reward yourself. If the goal is not measurable, you cannot tell whether you are making progress or not. If you have drinking water in a container, you will only be able to tell whether it is enough for ten people when you know its quantity. By establishing the quantity, you are able to make a decision. It is the same with a goal. Until you are able to measure a goal, your success is blocked and not easily achieved. A goal needs to be **achievable.** It is equally important to set a goal that is not out of this world. Setting goals that cannot be met with the resources and abilities that one has does not add value and ends up in frustration. I can choose to set a goal to tour five African nations in the next two weeks. Although this is possible, it might not be achievable in view of my work schedule and available cash. Someone might question my level of faith but I would in turn challenge their wisdom in setting the said goal. This brings us to the next point - a goal needs to be **realistic**. We should not set goals for the sake of doing so. A goal needs to be possible, and specifically, possible to me. Unless my job requires me to travel frequently and I have work that I need to do in the five African nations, it might not be realistic to try and do so.

Lastly, a goal needs to be **time-bound**. A goal without a time limit is hard to achieve because it is never due. There will never be urgency to have it complete neither reason to worry because it will never be late. A goal therefore needs to have a **time frame** in which it should be achieved to help keep us in check. Time frames help us measure our progress and give us a reference point when establishing our achievements. If I set a goal that every year I need to identify someone to influence and begin working with them (remember my vision is to positively influence one person at a time), I am able to tell whether I am making progress or not.

Therefore, every time I am reviewing my goals, I will consider where I am in regard to this goal. The first question I will ask is, have I identified someone? If I have not, what do I need to do to identify someone? If I have identified someone, then the next question will be, what level of activities have the person and I been engaged in? I hope we get the drift here. When there is a time frame set on any goal, it is easy to measure it and then establish whether any achievements are being made.

A goal also needs to be **flexible**. You will hurt yourself if the goal you set is rigid. A rigid goal does not produce good results mostly because one is tempted to deliver the goal without necessarily considering all the factors that affect the factors that surround the goal. A good example is that I can set a goal to complete reading a topical book within 30 days. When setting the goal, I might not have known that the topic being discussed is extensive and there are exercises that need to be completed. However, because my goal is to complete reading the book in 30 days, I could end up just reading through the book without digesting its contents or even doing the recommended exercises. I needed to be flexible when I realized the kind of book I was holding in my hands. On the other hand I am not implying that if you encounter an obstacle, the goal should be thrown out of the window and just continue with life as though there was no goal. When I say that a goal needs to be flexible, I mean that you need to allow room to adjust the goal but not put it off indefinitely or completely. The temptation to put it off indefinitely or completely is very high. If you therefore find that you have to constantly change your goals, then you are either getting lazy or your goal-setting skills need to be improved. If the latter is the case, I suggest that you look for a book on goal-setting or just Google goal-setting and get some useful information. Zig Ziglar, an American Author and Motivational Speaker, said that a goal properly set is halfway achieved. If on the other hand you realize that the issue is that you are just being lazy (which unfortunately is the case much of the time) then do not adjust your goal. There is a saying that if you do something for 21 days consistently, then it becomes a habit. If you make it your business to complete your set goal irrespective of your situation or condition, then you will do it. I therefore suggest that the first 10 goals you set for yourself after going through this notebook remain as they are. Do not adjust the deadlines set even if you amend the goals itself. Once you see the benefit of completing the goal, then you will be about to adjust or change deadlines without losing sight of the goal.

Something else to bear in mind when setting a goal is that when goals are **broken down** into small sections or portions they are easier to achieve. My vision is to positively influence one person at a time. One goal that I can easily set is that "I will positively influence someone at my workplace". I can achieve this goal by working on it as a whole. However, I can achieve it faster and with much ease if I broke it down in three segments. My first segment can be that I will try my best and make a friend in the next three months. You might say, Muthengi, why do you want to take three months to make a friend? One, I know myself, I don't make friends easily. Secondly, friendships that are not relational don't go deep. Lastly, if I take time to develop the friendship, the person will not feel like all I had was an agenda when making them my friend. My second segment can be to establish whether the person is teachable and a leader in another next three months. The fact that a person is teachable is important to me as the objective is not to just positively influence people, but to influence them in such a way that they can also influence others in a positive way. The third segment of my goal can be to spend time with them sharing and impacting knowledge in the area I think they need in a period of a year. A good example I can share with you took place in one of the organizations that I worked for. I met this young man, saw his potential and realized that he was capable of succeeding me. I therefore purposed that I will train him in such a way that if I were not there, he would be able to run the office. I can confidently say that after one year, I could confidently go on leave without fear that things will get out of hand. The fact that I have split my goal into three clear segments means that I can see the progress I am making and be encouraged to continue. This then brings me to my next point.

A goal achieved needs to be **celebrated**. Every time you achieve a goal whether in full or in part, please celebrate it. How do you celebrate? It does not have to be a big party that clears your savings. Treat yourself to your favourite chocolate or drink. Take yourself to the movie theatre and buy yourself popcorn while you're at it. If you love reading like I do, buy a book you have been wishing you owned. My friend whom I took time to train and impact in the office bought me lunch and a wooden carving of a Masaai man (a cultural group that has kept its traditional dressing to date in Kenya) to say thank you when I was leaving the organization. I had never directly mentioned to him that my goal was to positively influence him. However, he was able to pick that up and was grateful for the time we spent together before I left that organization. He helped me celebrate and it felt nice to celebrate the fulfillment of that goal with the person influenced.

Achieving a goal will not come easily. Byron Pulsier once said that "There is no short cut to success; it requires persistence, hard work and the ability to learn from failures.[22] The process of setting goals helps you choose where you want to go in life. By knowing precisely what you want to achieve, you know where you have to concentrate your efforts. You'll also quickly spot the distractions that would otherwise lure you from your course. More than this, properly-set goals can be incredibly motivating, and as you get into the habit of setting and achieving goals, you'll find that your self-confidence builds fast.[23]

Goal setting should not be restricted to one issue in our life. We should set goals for all areas of life. We should set goals for our career, family, spiritual, academic life as well as an overall life goal.

GETTING STARTED

1. What are your thoughts from this season and why?

_____

_____

_____

_____

THINKING THROUGH

Set four goals (based on your vision) that you will work on in the next six months. I suggest that each of the four goals that you set covers a different area in your life. One can be about your career, another about your family/marriage, another about your spiritual life and another about your life in general. Keep them simple and short. For each goal, break it into at least two segments and make sure it is SMART. Ensure that it has clear deadline. Remember we agreed that before we start being flexible in goal-setting, we first have to learn how to achieve goals. Therefore, the first rule is that the goals can be adjusted but the deadlines cannot be changed. If the adjustment will make it impossible to achieve the goal then let it stay in its current form. However, remember the words of Michelangelo, "The greater danger for most of us lies not in setting our aim too high and falling short; but in setting our aim too low, and achieving our mark." The objective here is to get the gist and form a habit. Let me give you an example of four goals I can come up with.

a. My Career – Train one person on how to handle everything I do in the next one year

- Identify the person in my team within the next 3 months

- Draw a program of the areas I need to train them in and do it in 9 months

b. My Marriage – Do a study on raising children with my wife in the next 6 months

- Discuss the thought with my wife and agree within the next 1 month

- Purchase the study and start doing it within 1 week of agreeing

c. My Spiritual life – Share what I have learnt from my bible reading with someone at least once a week

- Determine how I will do my bible reading and set a time to read the bible everyday

- Identify someone and request them to allow me to share my lessons with them at least once a week

d. My general life – To complete writing a book on personal visioning in the next 6 months

- Determine the outline of the book and write it down in 1 month

- Research on the different areas and come up with a draft in 5 months

Now it is your turn. Come up with your four goals. Your can share them with your team mate and have him or her critic them.

a. _____

- _____

- _____

b. _____

- _____

- _____

c. _____

- _____

- _____

Season Six

Finale

Remember failure is an event, not a person.
&
You cannot climb the ladder of success dressed in the
costume of failure.
Zig Ziglar
American Author and Motivational Speaker (1926)

As WE CONCLUDE THE SEASONS, let us once again revisit where we are coming from. A vision is a picture of the future that produces passion. Remember what we said about passion as defined by Curt Rosengren; passion is the energy that comes from bringing more of you into what you do. Simply put, it's being who you are and doing what comes naturally. It comes from being in alignment with what comes naturally. A vision is achieved through gifts and talents. Gifts and Talents are given to us by God according to our abilities. Core values stem from our convictions. They influence others, express beliefs, communicate what is important to us and inspire ones lives. Core values are our deal-breakers and if we break them, our life feels empty. Every individual has strengths and weaknesses. Strengths are our positive traits while weaknesses are our negative traits. A goal is an objective or a target that one sets for themselves. Goal-setting leads to success. However, a goal without a time limit is hard to achieve because it is never due.

I would like to echo the words of Zig Ziglar that failure is an event and not a person. Many times, you will fail to achieve your goals and feel disappointed in yourself. Remember that failure is an event. Let it pass, recollect yourself and move on.

If we do the activities in this notebook and thereafter revert back to normal life, it will have been in vain. What is normal life anyway? Is it that place where you just live and do things without a plan? I hope not. Let's make personal visioning our normal life. I would like to suggest the following three actions to ensure that you do not lose momentum.

First, I would like to challenge you to **review** your goals every twelve months. That way, you will be able to tell whether you are making progress, whether you need to adjust the goal or move deadlines. When I was writing this notebook, I shared with a few people what I was doing and the goals and timelines I had set for myself. I continued to monitor myself to see how close I was to completing my goal on time and there are times I had to spend several hours indoors or burn the midnight oil to meet my deadline. The more I reviewed my progress, the more I felt challenged to keep to the deadlines.

Secondly, you need to set **corrective actions** for any goals not achieved. It is not all the time that you will achieve your goals. I have not achieved all my goals this far. There are times I have had to suspend goals because they were not timely, others I have had to abandon altogether. However, as you review your goals, you might realize that the goal is not aligned to your vision at all or it is diverting you from your vision. This might require you to change course or even change the goal. Bottom line - you must correct the situation. There is a common saying in Africa that it is only a fool who does not change his mind. Let's feel free to change course as long as we do not lose sight of the goal.

Thirdly, you need to have an **accountability** system. Like I mentioned earlier, when I was writing this notebook, I informed several people of what I was doing and the timelines I had set. I did not ask these people to follow me up or even to keep me in check. However, because I told them of what I was doing and when I wanted to have it done, they would ask about my progress. That put me on my toes because I did not want to let myself (or them) down. Other times you might want to ask someone to specifically hold you accountable for your goal. A good example which would apply to a single person (who is dating) would be to set a goal such as, "I will remain pure until I get married". This is one of those goals you would do well to ask someone to hold you accountable to, possibly in defined intervals. You may ask them to look you straight in the eye and ask whether you have had sex with your significant other. This knowledge that you are accountable to someone will help make it hard for you to change your mind about your goal or let yourself get into compromising situations.

GETTING STARTED

1. What are your thoughts from this season and why?

_____

_____

_____

_____

DIGGING DEEPER

2. For the four goals that you set, indicate a review period for them. I propose that you come back twelve months from this date and review them.

    a. Date_____Goal _____

          i. _____

          ii. _____

    Achievements - Date

          i. _____

          ii. _____

    b. Date_____Goal _____

          i. _____

          ii. _____

    Achievements - Date

          i. _____

          ii. _____

    c. Date_____Goal _____

          i. _____

          ii. _____

Achievements - Date

    i. _____

    ii. _____

d. Date_____Goal _____

    i. _____

    ii. _____

Achievements - Date

    iii. _____

    iv. _____

3. Let's now list our accountability systems. I suggest that for these four goals you actually get people and ask them to hold you accountable.

    a. _____

    Accountability System

    _____

    b. _____

    Accountability System

    _____

c. _____

Accountability System

_____

d. _____

Accountability System

_____

Conclusion

I don't want to get to the end of my life and find out
that I lived just the length of it. I want to have lived the
width of it as well.

Diane Ackerman[24]

SIX SEASONS DOWN, IT WILL be very unfortunate if all you did was
just read through this notebook. The benefits of this notebook
can only be realized when you complete the exercises. If by any
chance you have managed to get through this notebook without
doing the exercises, I implore you to please go back and complete
them.

I conclude this notebook with several quotes from a book
by John Maxwell and Jim Dornan titled "Becoming a Person of
Influence"[25] which summarizes the six seasons we have gone
through.

For most people, it's not what they are that holds them back.
It's what they think they are not. Pg 52

Don't let yourself be pressured into thinking that your dreams
or your talents aren't prudent. They were never meant to be
prudent. They were meant to bring joy and fulfillment into your
life. Pg 131

We grow by dreams. All big (individuals) are dreamers. They
see things in the soft haze of the spring day or in the red fire on a
long winter's evening. US President Woodrow Wilson Pg 132

Some of us let those great dreams die, but others nourish and
protect them; nourish them through bad days until they bring
them to the sunshine and light which comes always to those who
sincerely hope that their dreams will come true. Pg 189

Every situation, properly perceived becomes an opportunity. (A quote from Authors Helen Schucman and William Thefford) Pg 127

Passion is the fuel that helps people nourish and protect their dreams. Pg 189

We've been told that in hospital emergency rooms, nurses have a saying: "Watch one, do one, teach one". It refers to the need to learn a technique quickly, jump right in and do it with a patient, and then turn around and pass it on to another nurse. Pg 209

It would be nice to move the personal visioning process to another level. Do it for your family. Go through the same process with your wife or husband and write a family vision, family values, and goals.

I have attached a template which you should feel free to make as many copies of as you need. I hope your life is changed. However, if you do not review your goals, put in place corrective measures where necessary and have accountability systems, the possibility of success is very low.

My Personal Vision

Name _____ Date _____

My Vision is: _____

My Gift and Talents are:

1.   ....

2.   ....

3.   ....

4.   ....

My Values are:

1.   ....

2.   ....

3.   ....

4.   ....

My Strength:

1.   ....

      a.   How do I improve it?

2.   ....

      a.   How do I improve it?

My Weakness:

1.   ....

      a.   How do I watch it?

2. ....

      a.   How do I watch it?

My Goals are:

Date: _____

Goal 1 _____

Date achieved _____

Goal 2 _____

Date achieved _____

Goal 3 _____

Date achieved _____

Goal 4 _____

Date achieved _____

My Auxiliary Vision is: _____

Family / Marriage/ Spiritual Life/ Career

Vision _____

Values

1. ....

2. ....

3. ....

4. ....

Goals

1. ....

2. ....

3. ....

Notes

(Endnotes)

1   History of Steve Jobs retrieved on 24112010 from www.answers.com/topic/steve-jobs

2   History of Steve Jobs retrieved on 24112010 from www.noteablebiographies.com/Ho-Jo/Jobs-Steve.html

3   History of Martin Luther Jr. retrieved on from http://www.americanrhetoric.com/speeches/mlkihaveadream.htm

4   Hybels, Bill. (2004). "Courageous Leadership." Grand Rapids, Michigan 49530 USA: Zondervan, 2002. (P 21)

5   Rosengren, C. (2004). The Occupational Adventure Guide – A travel guide to the career of your dreams. (P 20)

6   Matthew 25:14-30

7   W.B.Freeman Concepts, Inc (1999). "God's little lessons on life for Mom" Tulsa, Oklahoma: Honor Books. (P 193)

8   Coca cola Company. Vision statement as retrieved on 03092010 from http://www.thecoca-colacompany.com/ourcompany/mission_vision_values. html

9   Unilever East and Southern Africa. Vision statement as retrieved on 03092010 from http://www.unileveresa.com/aboutus/purposeand_principles/?WT.LHNAV=Purpose_&_principles

10 International Christian Centre's Strategic plan (2010-14). A vision to die series.

11 Malphurs, A. (2006). Advanced Strategic Planning: A new Model for Church and Ministry Leaders. Grand Rapids: Bakers Books. (P 96)

12 State of Iowa (1999). Guide for State Agency Strategic Planning.

13 Malphurs, A. (2006) Advanced Strategic Planning: A new Model for Church and Ministry Leaders. Grand Rapids: Bakers Books. (P 96 – 100)

14 Genesis Chapters 37 - 41
15 International Christian Centre's Strategic plan (2010-14). A vision to die series.
16 Harding, A. (2010, Aug). Writing on Rwanda. Retrieved on 04062010 from http://www.bbc.co.uk/blogs/thereporters/andrewharding/2010/08/rwanda.html
17 Definition of personality as retrieved on 13092010 from http://www.answers.com/topic/personality
18   Definition of personality as retrieved on 13092010 from http://wfnetwork.bc.edu/glossary_entry.php?term=Personality,%20Definition%20of&area=All retrieved on 13092010
19 Description of the traditional four temperaments as retrieved on 13092010 from http://www.personalitypage.com/html/four-temps.html
20 Keirsey, D. Description of temperaments. Retrieved on 14092010 from http://www.keirsey.com/handler.aspx?s=keirsey&f=fourtemps&tab=1&c=overview retrieved on 14092010
21 Description for goal setting as retrieved on 21092010 from http://www.mindtools.com/page6.html
22 Description for goal setting as retrieved on 21092010 from http://www.goal4success.com/
23 Description for goal setting as retrieved on 21092010 from http://www.goal4success.com/ retrieved on 21092010
24 Burgess t, Pugh K & Sevigny L. (2007). "The Personal Vision Workbook". Thomson Delmar Learning
25 Maxwell J & Dornan J. (1997). "Being a Person of Influence". Thomas Nelson Inc Publishers: Nashville, Tennessee.